Visit

www.YoungerMeAcademy.com

to request an author visit for your organization, download free coloring pages, watch free video e-books, and more.

If you enjoy this book, please

Leave A Review ⟶

to support our independent family project.

Created by Ben Okon

Illustrated by Jeevankar Bansiwal

For Emmett and Averie, two wonderful sources of happiness

Special acknowledgment to Nobel Prize winner Daniel Kahneman and economist Amos Tversky, whose pioneering research on Prospect Theory inspired many of the insights in this book.

Published by Younger Media, LLC

www.youngermeacademy.com

ISBN: 978-1-961428-02-7 (hardcover)

Library of Congress Control Number: 2023910671

Emmett the Elephant played in his lake,
as he sat near its soft sandy shore.
He liked his small spot but the sun was too hot,
so he wished he could have something more.

He had a big dream of a river that gleamed
with tall fountains and water so clear.
He let out a sigh as a bottle bobbed by.
As he grabbed it, a smoke cloud appeared!

"Emmett, you freed me! I'm Averie, your genie!
I'll grant you the wish of your dreams!"

"Wow!" Emmett cried, "I know **just** what I'd like:
a big river with rapids and streams!"

Averie said, "Easy!" then waved her toes freely
as water sprayed up all around.
Sparks and lights flew as big waterfalls grew,
and a river emerged from the ground.

"Weee!" Emmett screamed. "But could this really be?"
With a splash Emmett started to swim.
He dove and he played as the waterfalls sprayed.
"Thank you, Averie!" he yelled with a grin.

But as days turned to weeks, Emmett's mood turned more bleak. "Averie, please will you grant me one more?

This river's sublime, but it's been a long time . . .
it's becoming a bit of a bore."

"You have such a great haunt, so what more could you want?
I'll help you, but please make it snappy!"

"You pick," Emmett said as he hung his large head.
"I'd like something that makes me more happy!"

With a flick of her wand, she turned river to pond.
It was simple and small, nothing more.
With a smile and a wink, Averie left in a blink,
leaving Emmett more sad than before!

He had wanted much more. This new pond was a bore!
He missed splashing around in his river.

But in time he grew fond of his quaint little pond,
and began to enjoy its blue glimmer.

Then one day, a surprise! The rain poured from the skies,
and splashed down from the side of the mountain!
The pond grew and grew and became something new.
The water flowed down like a fountain!

After a day all the rain went away,
so that Emmett could rest and get warm.

But each weekend or two a wild wind would come through, and give Emmett a wet, playful storm!

When Averie, his friend, came to meet him again,
Emmett told her how happy he was.
"How did you guess what would bring such success?
You deserve a big round of applause!"

"Over the years, I've seen wishes bring tears from animals asking for stuff.

They are glad for a bit, but their happiness splits . . .
when the newness wears off, it's enough."

"See, this lion has more than one lion can eat!
When I give him new food he might frown.

When I give it to jackals, they happily cackle,
and hungrily wolf that food down!"

"*You're right!*" Emmett said.

"I was happy while fond of my quaint little pond
and surprised once or twice with a storm.
Big waters are boring when rain's always pouring,
but special when out of the norm!"

Emmett's feet shook the ground as he danced all around.
He was now a true happiness master!
Averie waved her goodbye as she flew to the sky
And Emmett lived happily ever after.

"OLDER ME" ACADEMY

(More about Prospect Theory for adults and advanced readers)

If you've ever been amazed by a new toy or a big gift, you may have eventually lost that wonderful feeling that came from it (just like Emmett). Why? In 1979 Amos Tversky and Daniel Kahneman developed "Prospect Theory," a groundbreaking explanation that demonstrates that happiness is driven by gains and losses, not by overall levels of wealth, accomplishment, or any other final outcome. Among other things, they learned:

- **We all have a reference point,** which you can think of as what you expect to happen without any big change or outside influence. For now, pretend that your reference point is that you expect to get 3 gifts for your birthday.

- **We view gains and losses relative to that reference point.** You expected 3 gifts, so if you get 5, you'll feel incredibly happy. If you only get 2, you'll be a little sad.

- **The bigger a gain or loss, the less sensitive we are if it changes a bit.** If you get 20 gifts, you'll be ecstatic! But probably not much happier than you would be with 19. You'd just be focused on how happy you are to have a lot more gifts than you expected! It's the same for losses: if someone steals 15 of your 20 gifts, you'll feel about as bad as if someone only steals 14.

- **Losses hurt us more than similar gains feel good.** If you get 20 gifts, but someone steals them, you'll probably be sadder than you would be if you had never gotten them at all. And if the police find the stolen gifts and give them back, it probably won't completely make up for how bad you felt when they got stolen. You'll still be mad at the thief.

- **Our reference points change as we get used to new situations.** If you get 100 gifts every year, that will eventually become your new reference point. Next time someone offers you 5, it won't be as exciting as it originally would have been.

There are an infinite number of ways you can use this to maximize your own happiness. It comes down to embracing the simple things in life and, when you do need to experience loss, "ripping the band-aid off" and bundling those losses together. Want a fancy new toy? Borrow it from a friend for a bit, so you can enjoy it without changing your reference point. Planning a huge gift for someone? Consider surprising them more frequently and less predictably with smaller (but still meaningful and enjoyable) ones. Have to clear some space in your closet? It will be easier to get rid of a lot of valued belongings all at once than to give them away one at a time.

Fun fact: The "memory" part of an elephant's brain is larger and more dense than a human's. Perhaps that makes their reference points harder to change!

THE EXTRA ADVANCED "OLDER ME" ACADEMY

If you know how to read a graph, it can help you visualize what happened to Emmett. When Emmett was used to his small pond, he felt fine, but not particularly happy or sad (**Point 1** at the center of the graph). Averie then gave him a big, magical running river, which made Emmett happy and moved him upwards on the graph (**Point 2** at the top right of the graph).

On the next page, you will see what happened when his reference point changed.

Graph 1: Emmett felt OK at first with his small pond, but GREAT when Averie gave him a big magic river!

Higher: Emmett is happier

2

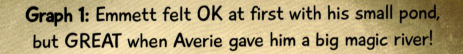

1

Farther left:
Emmett <u>loses</u> something greater

Farther right:
Emmett <u>gets</u> something greater

Center: Reference point

Lower: Emmett is sadder

Graph 2: When Emmett got used to the river, it became his new reference point. After that, the pond made him feel WORSE than before!

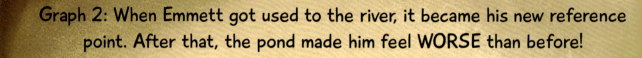

Higher: Emmett is happier

3

Farther left:
Emmett <u>loses</u> something greater

Center: Reference point

Farther right:
Emmett <u>gets</u> something greater

4

Lower: Emmett is sadder

When Emmett's magical river stuck around too long, it became his new reference point (**Point 3** at the center of the graph). After that, his puny pond felt like a huge loss (**Point 4** at the bottom left of the graph). When he lost something, his change in emotion was much steeper than when he gained something because losses hurt more than gains feel good.

After the river disappeared, Emmett's new pond, which was just like his original one, eventually became his reference point again . . . so when the storms came back, Emmett had a big happy surprise! However, it never stuck around long enough to change his reference point, so he was able to live happily ever after.

The Story Behind YOUNGER ME ACADEMY

Great children's books create special moments that can be shared across generations.

I realized this when my grandmother Gigi, a retired writing teacher, became isolated during COVID-19 with no way to meet my new baby Judah. Instead, we connected over video, where we enjoyed reading Judah's books together.

These moments we shared—the three of us, across nearly 100 years of age—were special, but usually not because of the books. Most books were written for *Judah* without reaching out to pull *me* into his moment as well. They taught him the ABC's, showed him pictures of new things, and told him stories about sharing and friendship.

But I wanted a book that I could learn from, too. In particular, I wanted to learn things that I wished I had learned when I was younger, so that Judah and I could grow together. I began writing my own books, and the *Younger Me Academy* was born. Each book is designed to:

- **Help anybody of any age learn and grow** with simplified life-long lessons from science, psychology, business, and beyond.

- **Pull everyone in** (including older readers and younger listeners) through vividly illustrated, character-driven stories written with rhythm and rhyme.

- **Create a deep, special moment** between easily-distracted kids and parents with stories that are long enough to savor but short enough to finish in one fun read.

Younger Me Academy is dedicated to Gigi. Through her writing, teaching, and stories, she inspired me to be a better father, husband, friend, professional, and human. My dream is that this series can continue her legacy by helping other growth-oriented families and their "Younger Me's" to do the same.

Thanks for reading. Please support this independent family project by leaving a book review wherever you found *Younger Me Academy.* I love to learn from you too, so I read every single one.

Ben

Ben Okon is a father who never outgrew his childhood habit of asking "why?" and "how?" Now that he has to be the one giving the answers, he loves challenging himself to think through the things he wishes he had known earlier in life from the perspective of a child.

In his spare time, Ben is a business leader who has developed people, product, and corporate strategies with companies like Google, Bain & Co., and Starwood Hotels. He holds an MBA from the Wharton School of Business at the University of Pennsylvania and a BS from the School of Hotel Administration at Cornell University.